Violet

By Alidis Vicente
Pictures by Nancy Cote

Violet

Written by Alidis Vicente
Illustrated by Nancy Cote

Published by
Operation Outreach-USA Press
Holliston, MA

ISBN 978-0-9792144-9-3

Printed in the United States of America

FSC
www.fsc.org

MIX
From responsible sources
FSC® C006892

To my mother, Madeline, who has always had a deep affection for the color violet. A.V.

To Missy, who like Violet, is filled with the dance of life.

Love, N.C.

There is a place, quite far away, where nature is untouched.
History and shifting times have not changed it much.

Long ago there was a day of chaos and divide,
That left two groups of birds forced to pick a side.

Nature lent its eye to watch the feud unfold.
Until this day, the tale has never been retold.

Care should be given to the lessons found within.
Now, my dear reader, the story may begin.

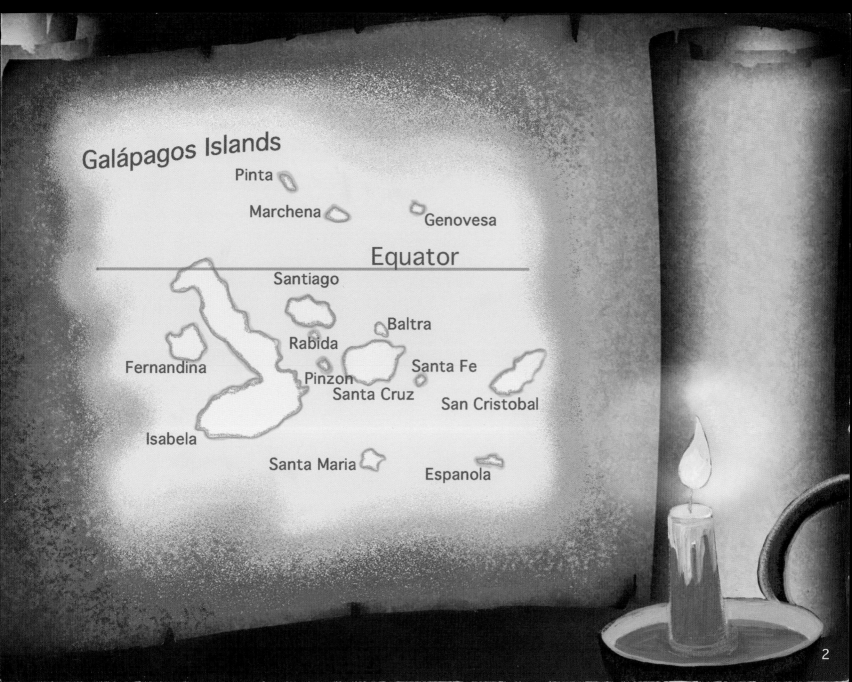

Galápagos Islands

Pinta

Marchena

Genovesa

Equator

Santiago

Baltra

Rabida

Fernandina

Pinzon

Santa Fe

Santa Cruz

San Cristobal

Isabela

Santa Maria

Espanola

It was told by a goose wandering at a zoo,
Who spoke to a visiting Australian Cockatoo,

Informed by a Brazilian Toucan strolling in the street,
That there once lived a bird with dazzling purple feet.

Violet, the Purple-Footed Booby, was one of a kind.

A product of two species that had never been combined.

They roamed a land off Ecuador's coast,

Known as the ancient Islands of Galápagos.

From mountain to rocky shore, animals ruled the land.

Sea lions crowded beaches, basking in the sand.

Dolphins and whales splashed in the ocean surf.

Flocks of bright birds soared high above the earth.

Violet's father, a Blue-Foot,
hunted at sea.
Her mother, a Red-Foot,
slumbered in a tree.

Blue and Red-Footed birds mingled
with their own.
Violet's parents found it boring,
wandering off alone.

Violet's Dad showed how a Blue-Footed dance was done.

Spreading wings and stomping feet, her heart he quickly won.

Violet's Mom charmed him with lovely crimson feet,

A jazzy, tapping shuffle and squawking ever sweet.

A family was started, combining red and blue,

Hatching a baby birdie with feet a purple hue.

Violet popped out of her shell, springing from the nest.
The world was her stage. There was no time for rest.
A Blue stomp inherited, along with wings spread,
Traditional dances turned on their head.

Hollering a squawk, Violet threw in a Red shuffle.

After another spin, her feathers began to ruffle.

Violet's parents marveled at the routine in awe.

It was time for the others to see what they saw.

Violet's family returned to their hometown.
The other birds sneered, staring up and down.
For family and friends was unexpected news.
A baby bird revealed, fresh from a snooze.

The crowd saw Violet, gasped, and covered their eyes.
"Her feet are....PURPLE! What a HORRIFIC surprise!"

A Blue asked Violet's mother, "What did you DO?
She's not one of US! She's not even one of YOU!"

The birds raged in protest, causing mass confusion.
Violet's parents worried there might be no solution.

Reds blamed Blues for the ugly mess at hand.
"Clumsy feet like those shouldn't be on land!"
The Blues rebutted, rants piercing the island breeze.
"This does not concern you! Go cower in your trees!"

Just when Violet's parents were about to run and hide,
A voice silenced the crowd with authority and pride.

"That's ENOUGH!" announced the Tortoise of Galápagos.
Plumes flapped in panic, huddling quite close.
"This is not who you are. Listen up here!
 You are ALL at fault! That much is clear."

Heads began to lower, peering at one another.

Violet was clasped within the wings of her father and her mother.

"The Purple-Footed One is different, but this is no way to act.

She is of both your feathers. Nothing can change that fact."

23

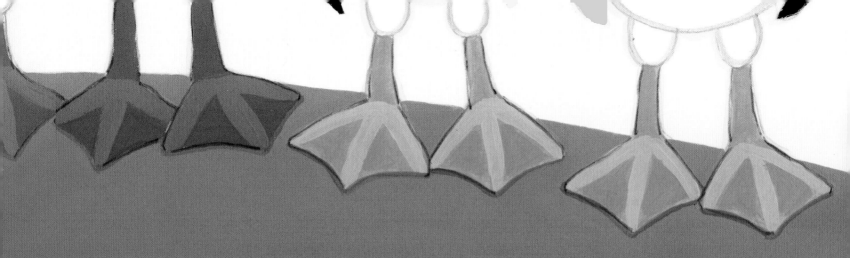

Tiny purple feet stepped out for the birds to see.

They did a dance, as others echoed with glee.

A Red noted, "Look at her dance! She is unlike you or I."

"Then", said a Blue, "Why don't we give it a try?"

Violet forgot the ruckus.

Nothing mattered at all.

With webbed-footed rhythm, she was having a ball.

Stomp, squawk, ruffle.
Spin a little spin.

Before long, other birds began joining in.

Violet's boogie spread with haste; her steps contagious.
There had never lived a bird so small and so courageous.

Each one tried the dance, and jived with every beat.

"THIS," said the Tortoise, "makes the Galápagos complete."

The birds gave the most vibrant show ever seen
With blue and red feet twirling, purple in between.

That day, birds with feet of sapphire and ruby

Were united by Violet, the Purple-Footed Booby.

Glossary

Chaos - a noisy scene of complete confusion
*pronounced   "kay-oss"

Cockatoo - any of various large, noisy birds in the parrot family that have a bunch of feathers on top of the head

Debut - a first public appearance
*pronounced "day-bue"

Galápagos Islands - island group belonging to Ecuador located in the Pacific Ocean, 600 miles West of South America
*pronounced   "ga-la-pa-goes"

Inherited - traits passed on by parents to their offspring

Mingled - to come into contact with others, or to combine with something else

Rhythm - a movement or activity in which an action repeats regularly
*pronounced   "ri-them"

Ruckus - a noisy commotion

Sapphire - a clear bright blue precious stone; a deep purplish blue
*pronounced   "sa-fire"

Tortoise - a slow-moving, land-based reptile with a hard shell.
*pronounced   "tor-tiss"

Toucan - any of a family of mostly fruit-eating birds of tropical America with brilliant coloring and a very large bill
*pronounced "too-can"

United - to come together to form a single unit; to join in action and act as if one

Vibrant - having or giving a sense of life, vigor, or activity

About Operation Outreach-USA

Operation Outreach-USA (OO-USA) provides free literacy and character education programs to elementary schools across the country.

Because reading is the gateway to success, leveling the learning field for at-risk children is critical. By giving books to children to own, confidence is built and motivated readers are created. OO-USA selects books with messages that teach compassion, respect, and determination. OO-USA involves the school and the home with tools for teachers and parents to nurture and guide children as they learn and grow.

More than one million children in schools in all fifty states have participated in the program thanks to the support of a broad alliance of corporate, foundation, and individual sponsors.

To learn more about Operation Outreach-USA and how to help, visit www.oousa.org, call 1-800-243-7929, or email info@oousa.org.